Fore

By Julie Nelson

STECK-VAUGHN
ELEMENTARY · SECONDARY · ADULT · LIBRARY

A Harcourt Company

www.steck-vaughn.com

Library of Congress Cataloging-in-Publication Data is available upon request.

Printed and bound in the United States of America
10 9 8 7 6 5 4 3 2 1 W 04 03 02 01

Photo Acknowledgments
Corbis, 26; Andrew Brown/Ecoscene, 8; Bob Rowan/Progressive Image, 11; Gary Braasch, 13; W. Cody, 14; Raymond Gehman, 17; Dewitt Jones, 24
Digital Stock Photos, title page, 4, 18, 20, 23
Photo Network/Craig M. Tanner, cover

CONTENTS

Koala bears have adapted to live in trees in the forests of Australia.

THE FORESTS BIOME

Some scientists study parts of Earth called biomes. Biomes are large regions, or areas, that have communities of plants and animals. A community is a group of plants and animals that live in the same place. Forests are a biome.

Each biome has a different **climate**. Climate is the usual weather in a place. Climate includes wind speeds, amount of rainfall, and temperature. Temperature measures how hot or cold a place is.

Different biomes have different kinds of soils. Many kinds of plants grow in biomes with rich soil. Fewer plants grow in biomes with dry, poor, or wind-blown soil.

Plants and animals are adapted to their biomes. To be adapted means that a living thing has features that help it fit where it lives.

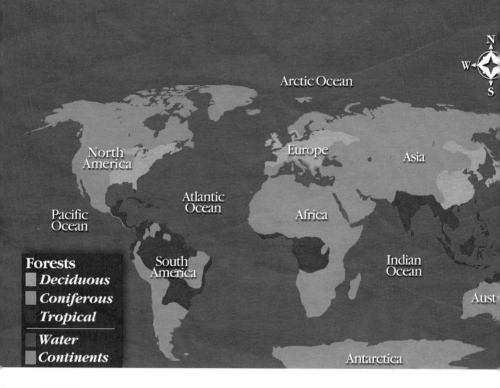

North America

Europe

Asia

Arctic Ocean

Atlantic
Ocean

Africa

Pacific
Ocean

South
America

Indian
Ocean

Aust

Forests
Deciduous
Coniferous
Tropical

Water
Continents

Antarctica

Kinds of Forests

A forest is a thick growth of trees and plants that covers a large area. There are three main kinds of forests. Each kind of forest has its own climate. Each also has different kinds of trees, plants, and animals.

One-quarter of the forests biome is coniferous forest. This kind of forest was named after the coniferous trees that grow there. **Conifers** grow cones that contain seeds. These trees have needles instead of leaves. Most coniferous forests grow in areas with cold climates and little rainfall. Some coniferous forests grow in temperate climates. A temperate climate does not have very hot or very cold temperatures. Coniferous forests grow in northern areas of Canada, Europe, and Asia. Other names for coniferous forests are taiga or boreal forests.

One-fourth of the forests biome is deciduous forest. This kind of forest was named after the **deciduous** trees that grow there. A deciduous plant has leaves that change color, fall off, and grow back again each year. These forests grow in areas with mild temperatures where rain or snow falls throughout the year. Deciduous forests are found in eastern North America and parts of Russia, Europe, Japan, and Asia.

About one-half of the forests biome is tropical forest. This kind of forest is named after its hot and wet tropical climate. Most tropical forests grow along the **equator**. The equator is an imaginary line that circles Earth and divides it into a northern and a southern half. Tropical forests cover parts of South and Central America, Southeast Asia, Africa, New Zealand, and Australia.

These vines are growing on trees in the forest canopy.

About Forests

Forests only grow in areas that receive enough water throughout the year. This water can be in different forms, including fog, rainfall, and snow.

Forests cover many kinds of land. They can grow on mountains, hills, or flat places.

Each forest has different layers. The emergent layer is made of the tops of tall trees. The next layer is an area of thick leaves and branches called the canopy. The canopy blocks a lot of sunlight from reaching lower layers of the forest.

The subcanopy layer is made of short trees that grow under the canopy. The shrub layer is made of bushes that grow lower than the subcanopy trees. The herb layer is made of short plants growing on the forest floor.

Soil

The floor of forests can be rocky or sandy. The soil may be brown, black, or red. On mountainsides, trees find places to grow where soil has collected in cracks in rock.

Forests grow best in soil that contains a lot of humus. Humus is made mainly of rotting plants and some animal remains. Humus has many **nutrients**. A nutrient is something that helps living things grow. Trees need nutrients from soil to grow. Humus also helps the soil hold onto water. Trees use this water to grow, too.

The soil of the deciduous forest is rich. Each year, deciduous tree leaves fall to the ground and rot. This adds to the humus in the soil. Plant life grows easily in this humus-filled soil.

Soil in coniferous forests is poor and sandy. Conifers have needles instead of leaves, and needles make the ground more acidic. This can cause the soil to be red-brown in color.

Tropical forest soil can be poor and contains little humus. In some places, heavy rains wash away nutrients in the soil. Many kinds of fungus grow in tropical forests. A fungus is a plantlike

▲ Fungi is helping break down this log into nutrients for the soil.

living thing that feeds on rotting matter. Fungus breaks down most of the dead plants in forests. Some common kinds of fungus are moss, mushrooms, and molds. The fungus of tropical forests breaks down dead plants so quickly that little humus is added to the soil.

Climate

Most coniferous forests grow in the coldest climate among forests. Winters are long and cold. Temperatures are below freezing six months out of the year. The short summers are warm and rainy. Summers last from 50 to 100 days. Some coniferous forests have milder climates. The Pacific Northwest rain forests and parts of the Pacific Coast in California are coniferous forests with mild climates.

Deciduous forests are warmer than coniferous forests. They have four seasons, including fall, winter, spring, and summer. They also receive more rainfall. The snow and rainfall is spread throughout the year. The snow melts in spring and supplies the forest with more water.

Tropical forests have the hottest climates. They also receive the most rainfall. Tropical forests can receive up to 400 inches (1,016 cm) of rain each year. Some tropical forests have high heat and rain throughout the year. Other tropical rain forests have seasons. The rainy season is the summer growing season when much rain falls. Little rain falls during the dry, winter season.

Broadleaf tree leaves change color during the fall season in deciduous forests.

Pine trees are common trees in coniferous forests. Their needles stay green all year.

FOREST PLANTS

The cold climate of some coniferous forests makes it hard for all but a few kinds of plants to grow there. These forests contain large groups of one or two kinds of coniferous trees, such as spruce, fir, and pine. A few broadleaf trees also grow in coniferous forests, such as poplar, birch, and ash. A broadleaf tree is a tree with wide leaves.

Most of the trees of the deciduous forest are broadleaf trees, including oak, maple, and elm. Shrubs, wildflowers, and moss also grow there.

Tropical forests are home to more than half of all the kinds of plants and animals on Earth. Some tropical trees and other plants include bamboo, mahogany, teak, palm, and fig.

Forest Plant Survival

Plants have adapted to the different forest climates. Some coniferous-forest plants must live in cold climates. Many trees there have conelike shapes to help the trees shed heavy snow. Branches covered with too much snow could break. The needles on conifers have a thick wax coating to keep them safe from the cold. Needles need less water because they are so small. They also lose less water so trees can grow in drier climates. Trees of the coniferous forest have thick bark. This protects the trees from the many wildfires that spread through the forest.

Plants in deciduous forests have adapted to warm summers and cold winters. The wide leaves would die in winter. So, they shed their leaves during cold winters to save energy. They grow the leaves back in summer.

Tropical-forest plants and trees face different problems. The lack of sunlight under the canopy layer makes it hard for shorter plants to grow. Many plants have adapted to find sunlight. Lianas are vines. They wind around the trunks

These epiphytes are growing on trees high in the canopy.

and branches of trees to reach the sunlight above. **Epiphytes** are plants that can grow on other plants high above the ground.

Some tropical-forest trees have smooth, thin bark. This may be because they do not need thick bark to protect them from cold or fire.

Grizzly bears are predators that live in forests. Predators catch and eat other animals.

Forest Animals

Forests are home to many kinds of animals. Large and small herbivores live in forests. A herbivore is an animal that eats only plants. Moose, deer, and elk are large herbivores that are common in deciduous and coniferous forests. They stay alive by eating plants on the forest floor. Squirrels, beavers, and chipmunks are small herbivores.

Large and small **carnivores** also hunt in forests. Carnivores are animals that hunt and eat other animals. Grizzly bears, wolves, mountain lions, lynx, and bobcats live in deciduous and coniferous forests. They eat herbivores and fish. Jaguars and large snakes hunt in tropical forests.

How Forest Animals Survive

The number and kind of animals depend on the kind of forest. The coniferous forest is home to fewer animals than other kinds of forest. More kinds of animals live in the tropical forest than anywhere else in the world.

Animals in coniferous forests and deciduous forests must be able to live through cold winters. Some birds live in these forests throughout the year. During winter, woodpeckers and chickadees find food under tree bark and live in holes in trees. Many other animals **migrate**. Migrate means to move from place to place with the seasons. They go south to find food and water during winter. They return north during summer when food and water are easy to find. Mice, groundhogs, ducks, geese, and reptiles are some animals that migrate.

Other animals **hibernate** during winter instead of migrating. They spend winter in a sleeplike state to save energy when they are hibernating. Animals that hibernate eat a great deal of food during the late summer and fall. Their bodies store the food and use it. They become active again during summer. The black bear is one animal that hibernates during winter.

The coat of some animals changes color during winter. Snowshoe rabbits and weasels turn white in the winter. This helps them blend with the snow. Then, it is harder for carnivores to see them.

How Forest Animals Adapt

Animals in deciduous forests must adapt to warm summers and cold winters. In the winter, they grow a thick coat of fur to keep warm. In the summer, they shed some of their coat. This helps keep them cool in summer.

Smaller forest animals have adapted to move among trees. Some of them have flaps of skin that look like wings. The flaps grow from their back legs to their front legs. They use these flaps to glide as they jump from tree to tree. Some tree frogs and flying squirrels have these flaps of skin.

Tropical-forest animals have adapted to live in the canopy. Some animals have special tails. Their tails are long and can grab and wrap around things. These animals use their tails to move from branch to branch. Their tails also help them keep their balance. Monkeys and some kinds of anteaters have these special tails.

Birds of the rain forest adapt by growing brightly colored feathers. Many birds also have special loud calls. Their coloring and their calls help them find other birds of the same kind.

This colorful parrot lives in a tropical forest. Its colors help it recognize other parrots.

These migrating monarch butterflies are resting on a bush.

Small Creatures

Insects are important to the life of a forest. Many insects live on the forest floor. Some beetles, ants, and springtails feed on rotting plants and animals. Millipedes and sow bugs also eat rotting plants and animals.

Insects are food for many of the birds and animals of the forest. Millions of insects hatch each summer in the wet ground of coniferous forests. Many birds migrate to coniferous forests to feed on these insects. They leave when winter comes.

Insects are also important to plants. They help spread pollen. Pollen is tiny grains made in some flowers. Most flowering plants need pollen brought to their flower parts. The flower parts use pollen to make seeds that grow into new plants.

The rain forest has more than 80 million kinds of insects. Mosquitoes, beetles, walking sticks, termites, and ants all live in the tropical forest.

Butterflies live in each of the forests. Some butterflies that live in the coniferous and deciduous forest migrate in the cold winters, including monarch and painted lady butterflies. Thousands of butterflies live in the tropical forest.

People use logs from forest trees to make paper products, such as toilet paper.

Forests and People

The forests give people many useful things. People hunt forest animals and fish. They mine underground metals and minerals. People clear the forest to build roads or towns.

Logging is a big part of the business of forests. People cut down trees for wood and paper. Wood is used as fuel or for buildings and furniture.

Many of the things people use come from tropical rain forests. Some plants can be used to make important medicines. Others are used to make clothing and furniture.

The rain forest is being cut down for its wood and many food items. Chocolate, bananas, and sugar started as plants in the rain forest. Even chewing gum began as sap in a plant called chicle.

Gray wolves are endangered because they are losing much of their forest habitat.

Today and Tomorrow

People overuse the products from forests. This causes too much **deforestation**. Deforestation happens when forests are stripped of their trees and plants. People clear forests to build farms and ranches. Farming, logging, ranching, mining, and wars can cause deforestation. Other causes are natural fires and disasters, such as storms.

Deforestation affects all living things on earth. Nutrients are part of the soil in forests. Without trees, fewer nutrients are added to soil. Also, rainwater runs across the ground much faster. This harms soil and washes away nutrients. It is hard for plants to grow in poor soil.

The tropical rain forest has the most kinds of animals of any biome. Much of the rain forest is being cut down each year. Rain-forest animals and plants may die out because their rain-forest homes are disappearing.

People are learning about forests and their importance. Forests help keep the Earth's air and water clean. Trees give the world more oxygen and water vapor. To keep the Earth healthy, they must protect the forests.

GLOSSARY

carnivore (KAR-nuh-vor)—an animal that eats other animals

climate (KLYE-mit)—the usual weather and weather changes of a place

conifer (KON-uh-fur)—an evergreen tree that produces cones

deciduous (di-SIJ-oo-uhss)—trees that shed their leaves each year

deforestation (di-for-uh-STAY-shuhn)—the cutting down of forests

epiphyte (EP-i-fyte)—a plant that grows on another plant

equator (i-KWAY-tur)—an imaginary line that circles the middle of a planet

hibernate (HYE-bur-nate)—to spend winter in a sleeplike state

migrate (MYE-grate)—to move from place to place

nutrient (NOO-tree-uhnt)—something that helps living things grow

Internet Sites

Educational in Nature: Forests
http://www.gp.com/EducationalinNature/topics/
   index.html

Live from the Rainforest
http://passporttoknowledge.com/rainforest/intro.
   html

The Wonderful World of Trees
http://www.domtar.com/arbre/english/start.htm

Useful Addresses

American Forests
P.O. Box 2000
Washington, DC 20013

USDA Forest Service
P.O. Box 96090
Washington, DC 20090-6090

INDEX